LOVE & WORSHIP:
A Lyrical Journey for the Heart & Soul

Simply Stacy

LOVE & WORSHIP:
A Lyrical Journey for the Heart & Soul

Printed in the United States of America

ISBN: 978-0-9887188-0-7

For my Mommy & Daddy
Juanita R. Poellnitz – 02/17/1947 - 07/12/1991
Joseph L. Poellnitz, Sr. – 04/28/1946 - 06/29/2012

You are the reasons the seed that was planted of me came
to be.
I love you both dearly!

Acknowledgements

I would like to first and foremost give an honor to God and my Lord and Savior Jesus Christ. It is because of Him that I was able to compose these words. It was His divine strategy and my simple willingness that brought forth what you are about to read today.

Secondly, I would like to thank my beautiful family, affectionately known as *My Fave 4*. Jelani, my covering and my love, thank you for being my biggest supporter. Thank you for always encouraging me even when I did not have the strength to encourage myself. You are my muse. A lot of the Love poems written here are about you. Thank you for being the epitome of a man, showing the world what God has in store for us if we would just be patient and wait.

To my beautiful children, Terrell, Sydney and Joi, you three are the reasons why I cannot and I will not stop. I do this for you. I love you more than words can convey.

Special Mentions

Joseph and Juanita Poellnitz – Though you are not here physically, spiritually I believe with everything in me that God will deliver this message from my heart to yours personally. Thank you for being the best parents ever. Everything you gave me sprung forth what is being produced today. I do this for God and I do this for you. See, we don't have to be overcome by our circumstances. We can, overcome them instead. Thank you. I miss you with all my heart and I love you both FOREVER.

Bridgette Hallman – It seemed like you popped into my life out of nowhere. But, God knew exactly what He was doing when He placed you on my journey. You consistently said to me, *"You need to write a book. This poetry is amazing."* I would laugh it off, never actually taking you seriously. But, God continued to use you to remind me of what He placed in me to do. Thank you for being a great friend, a wonderful supporter and a servant to God. It was your obedience to Him that caused you to continuously remind me of what I needed to be doing.

Laticia Salter and *Shawntae Kelley* – I did it! FINALLY, I wrote the book. You both never let me forget with every poem you read that you couldn't wait until the book comes out. You put the "S" in the word support. Thank you for believing in me and being some of the best friends for which a girl could ask.

My Butterflies: Tamala Booker, Melisha Calloway, Candace Cardoza, Mertha Gonzales, Bridgette Hallman, T'Shara Irving, Viva Kinnie, Tonika Mahdi, Jolana McKelvey, Ruby Munar, Derrika Ragsdale, LaFawndra Russell, Laticia Salter, and Karena Smith – You all are the BESTEST friends for which a girl could ever ask. Each of you played a specific part in my getting this book completed. For that, I thank you. Thank you for defining what friendship really means and for increasing the value of me. I love you ladies.

TJ Nicole – Finally, I would be remiss not to sincerely thank my friend, author, poetess, Ms. TJ Nicole of *Lillian Loveday & Company* for your help in providing me the resources I needed to get this project that was much bigger than me completed. Your book, *The Rebirth: A Woman's Poetry* inspires me tremendously. Thank you for being you.

Table of Contents

Love...

1. A profoundly tender, passionate affection for another person.
2. A feeling of warm personal attachment or deep affection, as for a parent, child, or friend.
3. Sexual passion or desire.
4. A person toward whom love is felt; beloved person; sweetheart.
5. Used in direct address as a term of endearment, affection, or the like.

"It is my belief that everybody needs love.
Love IS available to every heart that opens itself up to it."

- *Simply Stacy*

I'm Addicted

I'm addicted to you
This is true
Hi My name is _____
And I'm addicted to you know who

Your kiss, hugs, touch, and scent
Nights with you well spent
Moments I memorize
Never to end
You are so much more
Than my boyfriend

Romantically unique
Masculine and sweet
Perfectly molded
The MAN for me

Eyes for eyes
Hands for hands
The beats of my heart
Are rhythmic to the touch of this man

I'm an addict...

What Will Be Will Be <Or So You Think>

You're a pressure point for me
Leaving me in a state of disbelief
Imagining versus what's happening
What's next, for you and me?

Tired of the questions
Uncertainty doesn't sit well with me
I dismiss the saying, what will be will be
When it comes to what "our" future will see

Love, you won't admit
Singleness, you just don't seem to get
I hope you don't think I'll just sit
And wait for you, like your patient pet

Your heart will NEVER experience
Another love like mine
Your mind's interference
Will cause you to lose out
On the GREATEST journey
Of your love life's timeline

Hey Mister, you may want to wake up and see
That you'll never find another "lady" like me
I said lady, specifically
Because many can be born women
But I am a lady, authentic, unique

You may want to assess
The time you're taking to analyze
You and me
Before you're stuck in a rut
With the phrase playing over and over in your head
"What will be will be..."
And what's left will be NO ME

It Is With You

She's laughing
He smiles
Her hands trembling
Like that of a frightened child

He strokes her face
Stares deep into her eyes
Her heart slows its pace
While she crosses her legs, clinching her thighs

He softly begins to speak
It is you, that I long to see
It is you, that I want to spend life with me
Not as my girl, or just the mother of my child
But as my wife
It is with you that I want to walk the miles

My life has meaning, this is true
But my life would have an even greater purpose
If I have you
So today the games cease
As I get down on not one but both knees
To ask you, my lovely
To marry me

Inspire

There's a lot I have to do
All this business is because of you
You
Inspire me to go higher
Stretch wider
You are the gas
That lit my fire
Because of you
What you do
How you encourage me
To go on through
I'm inspired to be a better me
Because of the love
I receive from you

You tickle my fancy
Tantalize me too
I look forward to the moments
When I'm given the honor
Of connecting with you

Your kisses warm my soul
Your hugs shield me from the cold
Your words speak mysteries untold
Your love fills the empty holes
Once held by my heart

You inspire me
You require me
To be
The best woman
Lover
Wife
Friend
I could ever be
You inspire me

A Heart's Wish

My heart wishes
It would all go away
My mind wishes
Thoughts of you
Would find a new place to stay

Counting down
Backwards from 10
Wishing them gone
Only for them
To show up again

Love Slipped

Love slipped out of my lips
Your heart took a dip
But in the midst
You ripped the idea of you and me
From my grip
Love wasn't what you were seeking
Companionship was not what you needed
It was fun and fantasy that your heart was breeding
And it was the ignorance of me
That left my heart bleeding
Love slipped

The Deal

It's funny how we are
Talking in riddles, metaphors
Referencing each other by names like
"You're my star. I'd travel the galaxy to get to where you are..."

But when it's time to deal with reality
You and me, we should be on reality TV
Back and forth, up and down
Here and there, round and round

Either we're going to pick up this ball and play
Or put it down
Something needs to be done
In my Change Faces voice,
"Let's stop Fooling Around."

Tricks are for kids, games are too
Either it is or it isn't
What's the DEAL with me and you?

Love...FOREVER MORE

Wrapped in the prettiest of paper
Adorned with a lovely bow
Hand tied carefully
So that the receiver could truly know
How very special this gift is

Delicately delivered
With the utmost of care
A journey trailed by tears and fear
This giver's cross it bears

To the hands of the receiver
The package is delicately placed
In the moonlight's shadow
Stands a giver
Warm tears streaming down her face

A shallow breeze covers the moment
As soft, but slight words drip from the givers lips
"To you this day, I give my heart."
"Handle it with ease."
"I give because you stood apart."
"Do with it, what you please..."

"I'm giving you a part of me."
"That I hold fragile and dear."
"Please don't steal my heart from me."
"I can't shed another tear..."

Trust was the giver's issue
And rightly so
Pains, strains, bruises and bleeds
True love is what this heart desires to know

Stepping out on faith
Taking a leap like never before

To give their heart one more time
In hopes of obtaining the stamp labeled
LOVE...FOREVER MORE

Trust and loyalty is key...people need to be careful with their use of the word LOVE.

Sealed

You are the one
Who
Makes my palms sweat
My heart skip a beat
You are the one
Who has locked me in
For eternity
Your love sealed me
You cover me
You pray for me
You're just what my heart needs

Love Is Real

The way I feel about you
Leaves me feeling some kinda way
When I think about you
My heart seems to want to fly away

To spend forever with you would be ideal
How much I love you
Your love is so real

Lying in your arms
Loving your charm
I'm thankful for a love so sweet
A true love, that swept me off my feet

Destiny fulfilled
Sweetness I feel
For you, I have a zeal
Your love is so real

An Experience

Spaces in my mind
Emotions suspended in time
Leaving memories behind
That has me humming in rhyme

Incredible
Amazing
Mind-blowing
Life-changing
An experience

You fed me
Your touch read me
You led me
To a place my body thought
It would never be

An Experience

Put It On Everything

What you feel
You ask yourself, "Can this be real?"
Heart palpitations
Sweaty palms
Nervous twitch
Your emotions are currently doing a switch
From friendship to covenant
You're setting your heart
On the idea of the rest of your life with him
Putting your heart on the line
Investing something more precious than money
Your time
It's no joke
It's as real as real can get
You're no longer his homey
Lover
or
Friend
You're his wife
Next to God Himself
You're his life
Take your position
Stake your claim
On his heart
Is tattooed your name
Putting it on EVERYthing you love

Can't Believe You're Mine

Still I stand
Frozen in time
Shocked in my heart
Can't believe you are mine

Strong in your approach
The epitome of masculinity
Yet you find the most delicate ways
To touch the inside of me

A heart so kind
Mind so sweet
A body so fine
It'll knock any woman to her feet
Best of all, you belong to me

When we touch
It's no holds barred
What means just as much
Is how well you hold
My heart that's scared

Got Right By Me

Smooth
Slipped in slow
Unbeknownst to me

Now I am here
Heart in hand
Ready and willing
To give it to this man

He wooed me
Wowed me
Grooved Me
And now it's hard to see
What life is like
Without him next to me

Longing – *Haiku*

Close my eyes
See you
Weep

Feeling Love - *Haiku*

Strong as a storm winds
Heavily holding down the heart
Free from tears, happy!

He Knows

He knows,
I hold him down
I'll always be around
He has red line access to me
There's no place that I am that he'll never be

He's my rock
I'm his shine
He holds my thoughts
Consumes my mind

My king
Who does his thing
I wear his ring
He makes me sing

He knows, we fit
He knows, he's it
He knows, his place
He's already won this race

My lover
My sweets
My beautiful heartbeat

He KNOWS

Letting Me Know

That moment you kissed me
Told my mind, body, and soul
How much you missed me

You touched my hand
Kissed me slow
Hugged me tight
Letting me know

Candles lit
Soft and sweet
Our bodies moved
To the music's beat

Your song to me
Is nice and slow
This moment I longed to see
Thanks for letting me know

MOMENTS

Warm, sensuous, close, sweet
A touch, simple touch
That sends chills to the soles of my feet

Sweet melodies whisper
Like perfume scented air
Moments we're together
It's like the world stops
And we're the only ones there

Beautiful softness
Warmth beyond measure
Feelings that have never been felt
Except when we're together

The sounds of strings, guitars
Horns and cymbals
Melodies we make
Melodies to remember

Time goes on
Life remains
From this day forward
I'll never forget
The way you said my name

Writing from the heart brings peace; writing from the soul allows release.

One LONG Day Away

Beauty - he said that's her name
Closing her eyes, it all felt just the same
His whispers
His touch
The way he kissed her
Meant just as much

The time that he's away
Hurts her the most
It seems like the longest day
She so desires to hold him close

He's on the other side
Mind wandering as he day dreams
That he's looking into her eyes
This shouldn't be as hard as it seems

He grips the pillow close
Inhales deep
Memories of her etched in his mind
He imagines himself with her
Until he falls asleep

I can't wait to play that sound
The one that only he can make
Soft and subtle
I plan to leave it all here for him to take

Tomorrow...ONE LONG DAY AWAY

Light In the Sky

She's my beauty
The song I love to sing
With every breath she takes
God's existence is even more real to me

My beautiful light in the sky

I know you're scared
Wondering, "What is he up to?"
Baby I'm up to nothing
But I'd love to have my heart
Filled to capacity by you

Don't be scared
You've NEVER had a love like this
I know you've been hurt before
But you've NEVER had a love like this

It is my goal to hold you
Love you, mind, body, and soul
To give a love so true
It'll pique your interest till we're old

You're my beautiful light in the sky
That I never want to dim
I understand your mind is asking why
But listen to your heart, she says
"I long to be with him."

Fulfilled

Train your mind
To know what's real
Train your mind
To not always want a "feel"
But instead train your mind
To be fulfilled
To identify love & all it is purposed to give
More than kisses, touches, and hugs
But installments that build a foundation
Of love
Deep within
The core of your being
Defining love, beyond your eyes seeing
To be full to capacity
Yet still have room
To receive more love
And for love to be given from you

There are moments in time that can not be captured by a picture frame; those moments usually bear the name of Love. Oh what a beautiful name, Love.

True Love

It's true love
Sweet, raw, imperfect
We communicate
It's the time we take
To learn, love and grow

Life happens
People too
We're held strong
By what we do

He loves me deep
With his heart, mind and soul
He doesn't make idle promises
It is with him that I want to grow old

Society said true love is dead
But I beg to differ
His love is like an elevator
Doesn't take me down but a lifter

What we have is true love
The perfect imperfection
What we share is true love
In hand with God's protection

Love You

To have a moment
Be alone in time
Stand in it
Listening to your heart
Beat in rhyme

Feeling every breath you take
Memorizing every move you make
Because tomorrow's not promised

Your life is precious
Like a priceless jewel
Live and love every second
Remember, there will never
Be another you

Hug yourself on the inside
Love on you too
How can you expect someone else
To do for you
What you won't even do?
Love you

Worship...

1. Reverent honor and homage paid to God.
2. Formal or ceremonious rendering of such honor and homage.
3. Adoring reverence or regard.
4. The object of adoring reverence or regard.

"Worshipping Him worked a lot of out of me.
I am who I am today because I learned to Worship."

- *Simply Stacy*

Who I Am is Me

Though I was born into sin
Shaped in iniquity
God's Word tells me
That's not my destiny

I'm filled with purpose
He's mapped out a plan
He's penetrating beneath the surface
All I have to do is take His hand

I don't have to accept the fate
That the world has given me
See Jesus died on the cross
So that I could live, FREE

Who I am is me
Human, fickle, filled with uncertainty
Who I am is me
Searching to find out how He sees me

You Are There

Where I once awoke with tears
Consumed with worry and fears
I now wake up smiling
Because I know You are close and near

I smile for no reason
Laugh in my dark seasons
Because I stand free and clear
Lord, I thank You for simply being here

Where times seemed hard
Endless beyond compare
I no longer bear the world's pain
Simply because You are there

There's Joy in my storms
Happiness in my rain
Smiles in my sadness
Peace in my pain

Many ask why
And I'm all to eager to say
I'm full to the depths of the sky
Because God knows my name

Some days just aren't right
Hard to stand and bear
I stand and continue to fight
Because I KNOW You are there

Lost A Friend

I lost a "friend" today
Not in the way you may think
She asked something of me
That I couldn't honor
Made my heart sink

Well, I told her I'd made a change
Given God my life
Decided that on this day
I'm gonna walk with Christ

She didn't seem to take it well
Not well at all you see...
She began to talk me down
Reminding me of what used to be

"I remember when you did this..."
"That and the third..."
"Now you've found Jesus"
"Silliest thing I've ever heard"

"You've changed?"
"You? Club hoppin', head boppin'"
"Man droppin', junk talkin', you? Changed?"
"Well, you can have your God and your Jesus too

"What works for you, may not work for me boo."
"To be honest I don't want it too"
"I feel a little sorry for you, no more fun"
"Y'all Christians always appear to be bummed"

I stopped her in mid-sentence
To share my story
Of how my life's test
Became my TESTimony

He rescued me
From death and destruction
All He asks of me
Is that I place no one above Him

He loves me in my messy state
So much so, He's patiently taking time
To get me straight
He makes life fun, burden's light
He takes all of my wrongs and makes them right

So, I'm not bummed
Sad or dismayed
Instead I'm glad
That He chose me this day

My life's going somewhere
High above the clouds you see
I'll be sitting at the foot of the Father
While He loves on me

This life we live is not our own
You'll soon realize that when you are alone
Walk away if I'm not your cup of tea
But be careful, so called "friend" of the words
You speak against me

The Bridge

There's a bridge
I'm crossing
With tears in my eyes
But I will keep moving

Some I wish to take with me
Some I wish to leave behind
Why won't my heart just leave it be
Lamenting before You O God clear them from my mind

A heart that's hardened
Is not what I desire
A heart that's pardoned
Filled with God's fire

This bridge I cross
It's rickety and rough
As I cross thinking all is loss
The bridge's foundation stands tough

Help me O God to make Christ-like choices
Clear out my mind's field
Silence the voices
When it comes to people in my life
Paths I take
Even my approach to strife
Keep my soul for my life's sake

This bridge I cross
I know, is worth the walk
This bridge I cross
Will take more than talk

"For I consider that the sufferings of this present time are not worthy to be compared with the glory which shall be revealed in us." (Romans 8:18, New King James Version)

How Much Can I Get Away With....and Still Be Saved?

What I'm giving
Will never be enough
What I'm living
Will never be as rough
As the cross you carried
The beating you took
And I have the nerve to ask you
Lord please, let me off the hook

Let me smoke and carry your name
Let me cuss, blaspheme without shame
As long as on Sundays I shout and sang
Let me know how much I can get away with
And still be saved

I know your word says ALL or nothing
But I'm not ready to give in
Selfishly, I plan to keep on ducking
Because I don't want to lose my friends
Here I am Lord, standing before You asking, once again
Let me know how much can I get away with and still be saved

Grace says, I can do what I want too, *right*?
Live my life, how I like…
As long as I ask forgiveness, before I go to sleep at night
Everything in my life will be alright, *right*?

CERTAINLY NOT!!
You *sternly* speak

Politely reminding my heart of
Romans 6:15-23

How much can I get away with and still be saved?

ABSOLUTELY NOTHING

He Created

God created me
He knew who I'd be before my mother carried me
God the Almighty created me

He knew the life I'd lead
The choices I'd make
The risks I'd take
He also knew ahead of time all of my mistakes
Yet, even that wouldn't shake
The Love He has for me

God created me
He KNEW who I'd be before my mother carried me
God the Almighty created me

We're human beings
This fact is oh so true
Our humanness has gotten the best of us at times
But God! Rescued us from that too

People won't forgive you for being human
Often forgetting that they themselves are too
All you need to concern yourself with
Is knowing that God has forgiven and He cares
Deeply for little ole human YOU

God created me and you
He had pre-destined plans for us too
The almighty God created us
To live a life that is full, giving, and true
Please understand, we have to make a choice
To allow Him to abide in us; see us through

The knock at your heart's door
That many choose to ignore
It's a knock that will change your life
If you allow it too

It's Jesus, the Almighty Christ
Chastening after you

So you're human, with this life to face
Choose Jesus
He wants to help you see the end of this life's race

Reflections

I met this girl
She seemed real sweet
But little did I know
This girl and I were destined to meet

She introduced herself,
"Hello, my name is Change,
And I've come to give you,
A new name."

"The Creator of Heaven & Earth
Placed priceless gifts in you.
He's set expectations
He has something new for you to do"

"So why do you walk this path,
Of being everybody else but you?
It's time for you to step up
And start doing you."

"Tell fear to step aside
Lack of confidence too
God the Father has given you
A task to do."

I looked at this girl
With tears formed and falling from my eyes
Staring at this girl
For what seemed like a long time
Before I realized
The eyes I were staring into
Were mine

I'mJusSayinLord

Dearly
Sincerely
You're Near Me
You Hear Me

God, this is not easy
I know You will never leave me
I just wish my eyes would catch up
With what my heart sees

Visions of Joy
Abundance of peace
Not being coy
Lord knows I need a release

If I never see it before I see it
I never will see it at all
Strengthen my faith
Before I fall

#ImJusSayin

"He who dwells in the secret place of the Most High Shall abide under the shadow of the Almighty. 2 I will say of the LORD, "He is my refuge and my fortress; My God, in Him I will trust."

God's Plans

I asked You to fix it
You flat out said, "No."
I asked You to make it all better
You told me to let the old go
At first I wasn't sure how to take that
Just walk away and leave?
What happened to forever?
Isn't that how it is supposed to be?
I almost conceded in defeat
Hanging my head in shame
Selfishly thinking of me
I wouldn't even glorify Your Name
Because You weren't doing
What "I" thought was best
I expected You to bless my mess
Boy am I glad, You didn't listen to me
Following my plan, that would've ended terribly
You know the end of the story
Continued to follow Your plans
In spite of interference from me
You didn't just fix it
You made it new
My relationship has a new life
Because You did what You wanted to do
The man I married years before
That man, exists no more
Instead the man that stands before me
Is a man after Your own heart
You transformed the old man
into the man You intended for me
to have from the start
Not only did You work hard on him
You wiped my slate clean too
Our oneness wouldn't exist; had it not been for You
Washing out the old ways of thinking
Bringing out the best in us two
Making me a wife worthy of the man who holds my hand

You and You alone are the Foundation
Upon which we stand
We are stronger than ever
All because of You
Intended to be together forever
Because Your plans ordained us too

Marriage is an institution that God holds in HIGH regard because it represents what He intends to see in the whole world people on one accord. It is impossible to grow in a marriage if you are both in a silo, doing your own thing, going your own way, you might as well be decorated roommates. It is never perfect, but it is worth it. You may not be walking at the same pace, but as long as you are walking together in the same direction, no one, no thing, can sever your ties. Trust His plans.

I Remember You

I remember You
The One that held my hand
When I whispered to myself,
"If they only knew..."
"What I'm going through..."
While praying really hard
There stood You

I remember You
The One who held me
When moments seemed hard to bear
The One that warmed me
From the coldness of my despair
I remember You

I remember You
The One that counted all my tears
The One that sweetly whispered to me,
"It is with Me, that you can leave your fears."
I remember You

You remembered me
When You gave Your life on that cross
You remembered me
When everything and everyone else deemed me lost
You remembered me

Thank You Jesus for Your memory
Every second of my being
Thank You Jesus for loving me
You make this life worth living
REMEMBERING

Ms. Understood <Yep! That's Me>

Ever said you feel misunderstood?
I used to say that
I used to believe that
But I don't anymore
Because not only am I understood
But I'm completely figured out
Not by man, but by Him

Many may not take that as much
But I take that as gold
Why, you say?
Because for years being misunderstood
Is a lie we've all been told

He understands me
He demands of me
To do the BEST at all
He's placed inside of me

No longer do I feel misunderstood
I actually feel like the little engine that could
I feel like I can do anything
With His strength and the Joy it brings
Now you can call me Ms. Understood!

"For since the creation of the world His invisible attributes are
clearly seen, being understood by the things that are made, even His
eternal power and Godhead." (Romans 1:20, New King James
Version)

The Reason

His Touch and my pen
Sometimes are ALL I need
To drizzle out the message
He's placed in me

Joy's my staple
Faith's my campaign
Truth's my foundation
Living this life
Believing in the Power
Of His Name

Whatever it is to be done
To me, in me, through me
Whatever He says will be
Will Be

I'm not always hurting
In pain
Or wallowing in shame

I've experienced more days
That were sunny
When I stopped trying to do me
And called solely on His Name

He's the reason
Why any beauty at all resides in me
When there's a change of the natural season
His unchanging Hand is always holding onto me

"Teaching them to observe all things that I have commanded you;
and lo, I am with you always, even to the end of the age." Amen.
(Matthew 28:20, New King James Version)

Unconditional Love

I don't worry like I used to
Sorrow is no longer my last name
I live my life to please You
Since meeting You
I am no longer the same

Peace is my sister
Joy is my bestest friend
Love is my husband
Faith is the foundation
On which I stand

All these gifts
You gave to me
All of my burdens You lift
To ensure me a life that's free

What is it You ask of me?
That I make oh so hard to do?
Put away the selfish seeds
And give my life to You

You died for me
Cried for me
Love me to the core
Yet at every turn I seek
To run out of the door

The door to shame, hurt
Anger and Pain
The door that clearly defames
Your Perfect Name

Tears I cry
Caused by my own hand
Fickle am I

This imperfect man

But STILL You seek me out
To cleanse me of my pain
Your still small voice cries out
Your desire to give me back Your Name

"You belong to me," You say
"I simply can't let you go"
"My Son died for you one day"
"His blood washed you white as snow"

NO GREATER LOVE

Just In Case

Just in case you forget
I'm the One that held you when you wept
Just in case you can't recall
I'm the One who caught you
When others desired to see you fall
Just in case…

Just in case you fall in need
I'm the One Who sows the seed
The One Who resides within
The Everlasting Father
Forever your true Friend

To you this life on earth has an end
With Me, your life will truly begin
I have Light that chases darkness away
With one Word from Me
Peace is guaranteed to stay

You'll never get lost
Guided by My Sight
I paid the cost
So that all your wrongs will be made right
Just in case…

Just in case your memory ails you
Remember I Am the One
Who WILL NEVER fail you

Why I Bless You

You said Seek
And I'll find
My praise, my worship
Belongs ONLY to You

There's a Peace
My heart needs
A calm
In my spirit's sea
That ONLY You can give me

Despise not small beginnings
Question not Your plans
Keep my eyes toward the heavens
Trusting in You...not man

Your timing is perfect
Your purpose and plans are too
My steps will forever be ordered
If I continue to follow You

Everything that I've been through
You've allowed
So that You could use my storm
Like a bomb to shut the enemy's camp down

My pain was my purpose
All a part of Your plan
My assignment was my sin
If I had not been where I've been
I wouldn't know what You could do
These are just a few of the reasons why
I...Bless...You

Let your conversation be without covetousness; and be content with such things as
ye have: for he hath said, I will never leave thee, nor forsake thee. (Hebrew 13:5,
New King James Version)

Remember You When

They say, "Girl, I remember you when...."
You drank, when they called you skank,
You could never hold down a man...
I remember you when....

You reply, "Key words – you remember"
Which means you see a change
Go ahead and remember
Drinking skank is no longer my name

They laughed with a hearty skeptic's grin
"Changed, huh...when did all that happen?"

"He gave me His name"
Made me a promise...
That if I follow Him
The life I knew would never be the same
I was promised a life more abundantly
He even promised He'd never leave

"Well, woopty doo for you...we don't believe it's true"
All the mess you were into?

"Notice all of the words you use are in past tense"
He's given me a clean slate; it doesn't have to make sense
He desired a relationship with me
Cared enough to clear my record away
Regardless of if you believe it's true or not
It doesn't matter what you say
His word is all I need to keep moving forward

If you remember me when
And have to remind me of "who I used to be"
That makes me smile, you know why?
Cause it could only mean one thing
His change is real and it's happening in me
So go ahead and remember....

Just Where I Am

Faring
Not failing
Loving
You daily

Heavy hearts
Salty tears
Slow to start
Stunted by fear

I know You know
The plans you have for me
I ask you show
Me just a little
Lord please, I'm desperate to see

Your ways are not my ways
Your thoughts are not my thoughts
When you closed Your eyes and died
It was my sin and soul You bought

Purchased me from death's hand
Delivered from the condemnation of man
The price You paid for me
No amount of money will clear
It is for You I live this day
The ONLY reason I'm even still here!

"Come to Me, all you who labor and are heavy laden, and I will give you rest." (Matthew 11:28, New King James Version)

Purposed

Can't believe this is happening to you?
Who told you it wasn't supposed to?
Do what you need to do
Watch God get His glory walking you through

This fight you fight
Ain't about you
Instead it's about the souls
He's got connected to you

Honor Him in what you do
Make Him proud
Stand tall and speak what's true
Say it strong and loud

He's counting on you
To come on through
You're strong enough
How do I know?
Because He strengthened you

Go on man or woman of God
Do what is already in you to do
Defy these societal and worldly odds
Watch God's Glory manifest through you

He designed you to do what you're called to do....so do it

"For I know the thoughts that I think toward you, says the LORD,
thoughts of peace and not of evil, to give you a future and a hope."
(Jeremiah 29:11, New King James Version)

A Brand...Called Me!

Uniquely created
Originally slated
Authenticated
I'm a brand called me

I don't follow
I lead
Copying others
No need
I need to be exactly
Who God created me to be
I'm a brand called me

Fearfully made
Foundation carefully laid
Plans in place
My sole goal
Is to put a smile on God's face
I'm a brand called me

Feeling good about me
Do you feel good about you?
Do you feel like you're specially made
To change the world too?
I'm a brand called me
Are you a brand called you?

Hanging On

It's like I'm suspended in mid air
Unsure of if You're right there
With me
So I look to see
Yea, You're walking right beside me
It's the process that seems to be
Getting the absolute best of me
I'll keep moving
I'll keep fighting
I'll keep pushing
I'll keep writing
See, what's deep within
Must come out
You'll carry me through
Without a doubt
Some call me eccentric
Others dramatic
I don't really care what they think
I've got to get out of this attic
Though I'm high, I feel like I sink
Pushing through, what some call a storm
I define this, as NOT the norm
The norm, is Joy in the midst of pain
The norm, is having a sincere heart
Being able to dance in the rain
I'll get past this moment
Soon enough
But I won't sit here and lie
This process right here
Is rough
My pen is my friend
My thoughts are my walk
My push is Your purpose
Going beyond just talk
I won't succumb to the death that calls me
I'll live to fight another day
Though feeling like I'm just hanging there

A whispers Word from You
Is all I need to get along my way

Meditation - *Haiku*

Moments alone
Spent with You
To find me

Selah

Faith-FULL - *Haiku*

Seeing You
Breathing
Living in Love

Step Out

Move forward
Do it today
Stand firm
Let nothing; not even you
Get in the way
Live your dreams
TODAY!

Energy Change

My energies changed
My thought process too
Things aren't the same
I'm no longer on the same path as you

I learned long ago
That everybody can't go
This day I take heed
To do what my spirit needs

No one man is perfect
No one woman is without flaw
It's just a matter of choices we make
Not about grasping for straws

Maturing, the growth process
Is not an EASY thing
But changing with God
Consistent joy, it will bring

Letting go of "relationships"
That were never meant to be kept
Opening doors and making room
For His gifts
Sending all negativity to the left

Want to see change?
It starts inside of you
You're made and STAMPED with His Name
A beautiful gift created that is you

Starting inside of me
Better than what I am
Is what I aspire to be
Leaving strain where it lies
Developing with a life in Christ

My Moments

My situation doesn't speak peace
My circumstances weigh heavy upon me
I truly want a sweet release
To put an end to the question, "Why me?"
Desperately
But to attain that
It will take more than me

Your word says to diligently seek You
Search deeply for Your face
Listen intently for Your voice
And while doing so, You'll provide us all
A measure of Grace

Well God, I'll be the first to say
I'm a little lazy in my search
Maybe that's why things are going this way

My moments are some kinda hard on me
Cloud my judgment, you see…
My moments lead me to believe
That I have no destiny
Again, I go back to Your word
You said you KNOW the plans You have for me
So I need Your help
Lord, HELP my unbelief

My moments
Lord, I've had enough of me
My moments
Decrease Stacy
My moments
Jesus died so that I
Could have that sweet release

I receive the sacrifice

The Blood already laid
Accepting all that's right
Resting in the cool of Your shade
Freeing myself of my moments
Filling myself with Yours

Through this journey I've learned that moments are needed; they remind us that we are never strong enough to live without God's Hand on our lives... I embrace my moments.

In Loving Memory of My Mommy

<u>She Interceded For Me</u>

From a place
Without a trace
Suspended in space
As the tears fall
I yearn to see your face

What I've never seen
You prayed for me to see
With no strength to lean
You secured a Foundation for me

Prayers in the late hours
Hugs in the light
Eternity in this life was not ours
You did your best to teach me right

Missing the essence of you
Wanting you to be
Wondering what I'll do
Without you here with me

You're walking pain free now
At the right Hand of the Father
I no longer ask Him how
He called home for His daughter
With tears in my eyes
Memories in my heart
I'll never forget where my roots lie
Or the blessing you secured for my start

Forever missing you in the physical
Praising God for your victory in the spiritual
Thank you mommy for giving me a reason to stay on the straight and
narrow
To see Jesus and you again soon!!

In Loving Memory of My Daddy

My Life Without Daddy

My father was the first man
To ever love me unconditionally
The mistakes he made in life, made me a better me
I love and miss my daddy, more than words can say
I'm literally taking the grief, second by second
I can't bear taking it day by day

I'll miss his worrisome calls
In the middle of my work day
When he'd call and I answer
Hearing him say, "Stacy, this your daddy..."
Like I didn't know who he was anyway lol

I'll miss the sound advice he'd give
That I wasn't always willing to receive
Only to do what he said and have it work out for me
I miss his laugh and the best part, his conspiracy theories
My daddy always did what he could to protect me
Because he always thought, someone was out to get me lol

I feel like writing right now, so that's why I'm here
I've cried so much, feels like my body has no more tears
Yes, I know, God has a plan
Yes, I know, God's ways are not like man's
Yes, I know, God will see me through
Still doesn't diminish the fact that I miss my daddy terribly
Daddy, what am I going to do without you?
Who will I become?
What will this change in me?

Rest In God's Amazing Glory

Juanita R. Poellnitz   Joseph L. Poellnitz, Sr.
02/17/1947 - 07/12/1991   04/28/1946 - 06/29/2012

Conclusion

It is my sincere prayer that this book of poetry blessed you, opened your heart and mind, eased your soul, did all that God intended for it to do for you. If it has, Mission One accomplished. Thank you for supporting this effort, I don't take it lightly at all. You could've sowed your resources into anyone, anything, and you chose to sow them into me, for that I am forever grateful!

It is my hope that this book prompts you to look deep within, explore your potential so that it may be birthed into purpose. We all have something IMPORTANT and IMPACTFUL to do. Yes, *including YOU*! Again, thank you from deep within for supporting this book!

Peace, Love and Blessings To You,
Simply Stacy

About the Author

Simply Stacy is a writer, poet, and motivational speaker who strongly believes that words give life. Because of that, she's mindful of what she speaks. Stacy is an encourager. She believes in empowering others and celebrating with them, too. Stacy doesn't take the platform of Spoken Word that God has given her lightly. She believes, therefore she speaks.

Connect With *Simply Stacy* –

Visit: https://simplystacypoetry.com
Follow: https://twitter.com/FollowingHisWay
Like: https://www.facebook.com/simplystacypoetry
Blog: http://simplystacypoetry.wordpress.com/